The Cool, Awesome, Simple Science Series

Hands-On Life Science

for Elementary Grades

by

Phil Parratore

Table of Contents

A Real Humdinger

1 minute

What You Will Do

Demonstrate that sound is created by air pressure over vocal cords.

Get it Together

◆ A partner

Procedure

1. Ask your partner to hum a song with his mouth closed.
2. Try to stop your partner from humming by:
   A. Covering his eyes.
   B. Covering his mouth.
   C. Pinching his nose closed very gently.
   D. Covering his ears.

A Closer Look

While you are humming, air passes over your vocal cords causing a vibration. Pinching the nose stops the air from flowing. Thus, the vibrations on the vocal cords stop, as does the sound. Only pinching the nose will stop the air flow.

3

Bacteria Boog-a-loo

5 minutes

What You Will Do

Model how quickly bacteria can multiply.

Get it Together

- ◆ 8 paper cups
- ◆ 1 lb. bag dried beans
- ◆ Marker

Procedure

1. Number the cups 1 through 8.
2. Place 1 bean in Cup 1 to represent the first generation of bacteria.
3. Place 2 beans in Cup 2; 4 beans in Cup 3; 8 beans in Cup 4; 16 beans in Cup 5; 32 beans in Cup 6; 64 beans in Cup 7; and 128 beans in Cup 8. Each cup represents a generation.
4. Calculate how many bacterial cells there would be in the next several generations if each cell continues to divide and double.

A Closer Look

Bacteria are tiny creatures making up a division of microorganisms, which are typically one-celled and can only be seen under a microscope. Some bacteria can cause diseases such as pneumonia, strep throat, Lyme disease, and anthrax. Approximately every 20 minutes, a bacterial cell reproduces by dividing into two cells. This is considered a single generation of cell division.

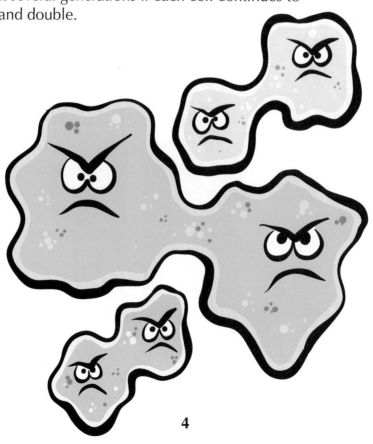

4

Be There in a Heartbeat

2 minutes

What You Will Do

Observe pulse rate.

Get it Together

- Modeling clay
- Matches
- Timer
- Table

Procedure

1. Insert the match into a very small piece of clay.
2. Flatten the bottom of the clay.
3. Place your wrist, palm side up, on a table.
4. Place the clay on your wrist, and move the clay around with your thumb until the match starts to slowly vibrate back and forth.
5. Count the number of vibrations that the match makes in one minute.

A Closer Look

As the heart contracts, blood is forced through the blood vessels. The blood moves at an even rate, causing blood vessels in the wrist to move. This is your pulse rate. Children have an average pulse rate of 80-140 and adults 60-80 beats per minute.

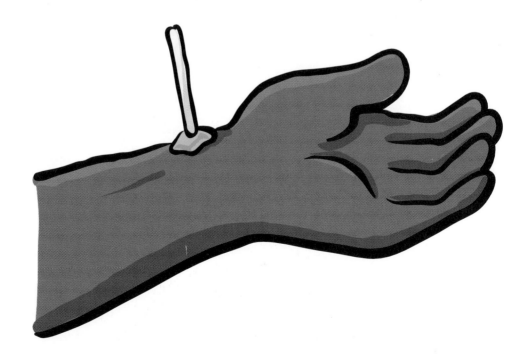

Body Parts

5 minutes

What You Will Do

Show the relationship of one body part to another.

Get it Together

◆ Yard or meter stick
◆ A partner

Procedure

1. Measure your forearm from elbow to wrist.
2. Measure your foot from heel to toe.
3. Compare the two measurements.

A Closer Look

The measurements of your forearm and your foot are almost exactly the same. Your body is made up of a series of patterns, just like in patterns you see in mathematics.

What Now?

Measure the distance around your wrist and your neck. How much thicker is your neck than your wrist? Stretch out your arms like a bird flying and have your partner measure your "wing span" from fingertip to fingertip. Compare this number to your height.

Anatomy
Coiling Intestines

5 minutes

What You Will Do

Model the size of your small intestines.

Get it Together

- ◆ Yard or meter stick
- ◆ String
- ◆ Paper
- ◆ Pencil

A Closer Look

All the string fits inside the square. The intestines consist of a coiled tube that extends from the stomach to the anus. Nutrients are taken from food as it passes through the intestines during the digestion process.

Procedure

1. Measure 25 feet of string. This is the size of the average adult's small intestines.
2. Draw a square that is 4" on each side.
3. Coil the string inside the square.

7

Don't Hold Your Breath

10 minutes

What You Will Do

Demonstrate the effect of hyperventilation.

Get it Together

♦ Stop watch
♦ A partner

Procedure

1. Hold your breath as long as you can and have your partner keep the time, in seconds.
2. Now, hyperventilate by taking 10 deep breaths.
3. Repeat Step 1.

A Closer Look

When people hyperventilate they add extra oxygen to their lungs and, therefore, can hold their breath for a longer period of time. After a while, carbon dioxide builds up in the blood, triggering the breathing response.

Attention!

Do this activity under adult supervision. If you feel dizzy during the deep breaths, stop this activity at once. If you have respiratory problems, do not do this experiment.

What Now?

Increase the number of times you hyperventilate after holding your breath. Also, try jogging in place for one minute before holding your breath.

Do Not Enter

5 minutes

What You Will Do

Demonstrate the digestion process.

Get it Together

- Coffee filter
- Spoon
- 1 tsp. cocoa
- 1 tsp. sugar
- 2 clear glasses
- Water

Procedure

1. Push your finger into the center of the filter to make a funnel shape.
2. Place the funnel in one of the glasses.
3. Fill the second glass about ¼ full of water.
4. Add the sugar and the cocoa to the water and stir.
5. Hold the filter in place and slowly pour the liquid into the filter.
6. Observe as the mixture drips into the bottom of the glass.

A Closer Look

The filter traps the undissolved particles of cocoa and prevents them from passing through the tiny openings in the filter. The water and dissolved sugar easily pass through the filter. This same process happens in your body. Digested food passes through the walls of the small intestines in order to reach certain body cells. Undigested food cannot pass through. It is moved into the large intestines and eliminated as solid waste.

9

Eating Heart Healthy

What You Will Do

Display how fatty deposits affect the flow of blood through an artery in the heart.

Get it Together

- Funnel
- Plastic jar
- Plastic knife
- Peanut butter
- Glass of water
- Toothpick
- Timer with a second hand

Procedure

1. Place the funnel in the mouth of the jar. The funnel will represent an artery in the heart.
2. Time how long it takes to pour the glass of water into the jar through the funnel.
3. Return the water from the jar to the glass.
4. Use the knife to spread a small amount of peanut butter along the bottom of the funnel's neck.
5. With a toothpick, carve out a hole in the peanut butter so that the funnel is partly, but not completely clogged.
6. Repeat Step 2.

A Closer Look

It took much longer for the water to run into the jar when the peanut butter was on the funnel. Likewise, the flow of blood is slowed when your heart's artery (funnel) is clogged with fatty deposits (peanut butter). If fatty deposits completely clog an artery leading to the heart, a heart attack occurs. When an area of the heart cannot receive blood, the cells in that area die. This permanently damages the heart. Limit the amount of fatty food you eat to help prevent clogged arteries and a heart attack!

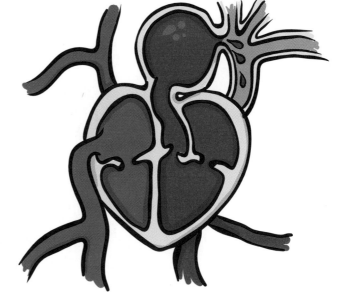

Clean Up

Use a paper napkin to scrape the peanut butter from the funnel. Then, put it in the trash.

Anatomy
Finger Power

1 minute

What You Will Do

Examine body mass distribution.

Get it Together

◆ Straight-backed chair
◆ A partner

Procedure

1. Ask your partner to sit in the chair with arms folded, chin up, and head high.
2. Press your index finger against your partner's forehead and ask your partner to stand.

A Closer Look

When sitting, all of your partner's mass is on the chair. To stand up, your partner's head must move forward. Your finger stops the head from moving forward, the mass from shifting, and your partner from standing.

11

Fingerprint Mystery

10 minutes

What You Will Do

Show how fingerprints are a useful tool for identifying people.

Get it Together

- ◆ Inkpad
- ◆ Several partners
- ◆ 2 sheets of white, unlined paper for each person

Procedure

1. Have your partners write their names on separate pieces of paper.
2. Have each partner roll one of her fingers from side to side on the inkpad and then carefully roll the inked finger from side to side on her labeled sheet of paper.
3. Choose one partner to make the same fingerprint on another sheet of paper. Leave this paper unlabeled.
4. Compare each labeled fingerprint with the fingerprint on the unlabeled paper.
5. Play detective and decide whose fingerprint it is.

A Closer Look

You noticed that every individual has a different fingerprint. No two people have the same fingerprints, which is why fingerprints are a very useful tool when trying to identify people.

Attention!

Ink can be messy and may stain. Wash your hands after completing this activity.

Gimme Some Skin

5 minutes+

What You Will Do

Examine how skin protects you from infectious diseases.

Get it Together

- 4 resealable plastic bags
- 4 fresh apples
- Rotting apple (leave sitting on kitchen counter for a week or so)
- Cotton swab or cotton ball

- Pen
- Paper towels
- Toothpick
- Rubbing alcohol
- Water
- Warm, dark place

Procedure

1. Label the four plastic bags 1, 2, 3, and 4.
2. Gently wash the four fresh apples and dry them.
3. Place one apple in Bag 1 and seal it.
4. Insert the toothpick into the rotting apple, remove it, and lightly draw the toothpick down the side of the second apple without breaking the skin.
5. Repeat Step 4 three more times, touching the toothpick to different parts of the second apple. Insert the apple in Bag 2 and seal it.
6. Repeat Steps 4 and 5, but pierce the skin of the third apple. Place in Bag 3 and seal it.
7. Repeat Step 6, but before you place the apple in the bag, dip the cotton swab in rubbing alcohol and swab the scratches. Seal this in Bag 4.
8. Store the four bags in a warm, dry place and observe every day for one week.

A Closer Look

The apple in Bag 3, which has broken skin, appears moldy. However, the apple in Bag 4, which was rubbed with alcohol, is clean because alcohol is a good disinfectant and keeps germs out. The apple in Bag 2 might have a small amount of decay, and the apple in Bag 1 has no decay. Your skin, like the skin of an apple, acts as a barrier against bacteria and infection. Washing your hands prevents the spread of germs.

Attention!
Wash you hands after completing this activity. Be careful not to get rubbing alcohol into your eyes.

13

Hands-On Hearing

5 minutes

What You Will Do

Practice your sense of hearing.

Get it Together

- 5 empty, black 35 mm film containers with lids
- 2 pennies
- Marble
- 1 Tbsp. salt
- 1 Tbsp. rice
- 2 Tbsp. water
- A partner

A Closer Look

Various materials have different weights; therefore, they sound different when shaken.

Procedure

1. Place the pennies, marble, salt, rice, and water into separate 35 mm film containers and snap the lids closed.
2. One at a time, give the containers to your partner.
3. Have your partner try to identify the contents by shaking the container.

What Now?

Try placing different items in the containers. Have a contest with several friends to see who can identify the most sounds.

14

Anatomy

Hot or Cold?

5 minutes

What You Will Do

Demonstrate that the skin is not always a reliable sensor of temperature.

Get it Together

- 3 bowls
- Cold tap water
- Room temperature tap water
- Hot tap water (but not too hot)

Procedure

1. Pour cold water in one bowl, room temperature water in another bowl, and hot water into the third bowl.
2. For one to two minutes, place one hand in the bowl of cold water. Place your other hand in the bowl of hot water.
3. Now, place both hands in the bowl of room temperature water. Compare the sensations.

A Closer Look

Your skin senses heat and cold and then sends a message to your nervous system. In the cold water, your skin sends a "cold" message to your nervous system. In the hot water, your skin sends a "hot" message. When you placed both of your hands in the room temperature water, your nervous system could not react fast enough to tell the difference in the temperatures. Therefore, both hands felt the same for a few moments.

Attention!
Do not make the hot water too hot to touch.

15

How Does it Feel?

5 minutes

What You Will Do

Test skin sensitivity.

Get it Together

- ◆ 2 sharpened pencils
- ◆ Tape
- ◆ A partner

Procedure

1. Tape the pencils together so that the points are even.
2. Ask your partner to close his eyes as you gently touch his forearm with both pencil points.
3. Ask how many points are felt.
4. Repeat Step 2, except touch the points to your partner's thumb or fingertip.

A Closer Look

You feel one point on the forearm and two points on the finger or thumb. This is because the nerve endings in the arm are too few in number to distinguish the separate pressures from the pencil points. There are many more nerve endings in the fingers, making it possible to feel both points. Fingers are more sensitive to touch than arms.

Attention!
Use gentle pressure when touching the skin with the pencils.

16

Anatomy

Human Genome Project

5 minutes

What You Will Do

Get a basic understanding of the Human Genome Project using a simple code.

Get it Together

◆ Pencil
◆ Paper

Procedure

1. Write the entire alphabet on a sheet of paper.
2. Number each letter, 1 through 26. Each number should appear under each letter.
3. This is your secret code. Now write your name using this code. Remember to substitute the number for each letter.
4. Give your coded name to another person and ask her if she can figure out your secret code.
5. Write short sentences in code and repeat Step 4.

A Closer Look

Imagine trying to crack a code that is 3.1 billion characters long. That's exactly what scientists working on the Human Genome Project are doing. Your genome is all the DNA packed into one cell of your body. Scientists estimate that the 23 pairs of chromosomes that make up the human genome contain about 60,000 to 80,000 genes. A gene is a segment of DNA that give us our own personal traits.

What Now?

Try to invent your own code and see if anyone can "crack" it.

I Can't Breathe

1 minute

What You Will Do

Illustrate what happens when airflow is restricted.

Get it Together

◆ Straw

Procedure

1. Begin by breathing normally, first through your nose, then through your mouth.
2. Place one end of a drinking straw in your mouth.
3. Gently pinch your nostrils closed so that you cannot breathe through your nose.
4. Breathe by inhaling air through the straw. Do this for 30 seconds.

A Closer Look

It was more difficult to get air when you were breathing through the straw. You needed to take deeper breaths and may have even felt a shortness of breath. This is how people who suffer from asthma, a disorder in which breathing passages become narrower than normal, feel much of the time. Also, people who suffer from allergies sometimes have the same problem breathing. An allergy occurs when the immune system is overly sensitive to a foreign substance not normally found in the body.

Attention!
Do not attempt this experiment if you have a respiratory disorder.

18

Anatomy
I'm All Bone

2 minutes

What You Will Do

Observe a model of a vertebrate skeletal system.

Get it Together

◆ Umbrella

Procedure

1. Open an umbrella and turn it upside down.
2. Examine how it is made.
3. While looking on the inside of the umbrella, fold it up again and watch how the braces and ribs collapse against the central pole.
4. Do this several times.
5. Think of what would happen if you removed the ribs from the umbrella and then tried to use it during a rainstorm.

A Closer Look

A vertebrate is an animal that has a backbone—like humans. A vertebrate's backbone is part of an endoskeleton, or internal skeleton. This endoskeleton supports and protects the body, helps give it shape, and gives muscle a place to attach. The umbrella has an internal structure that models a vertebrate animal.

Attention!
Use caution when opening an umbrella inside.

19

It's All in Your Mind

15 minutes

What You Will Do

Demonstrate the overlapping of images in your mind.

Get it Together

- White poster board
- Pen
- Scissors
- Hole punch
- Ruler
- Thick string

A Closer Look

You observe each picture as it passes in front of your eyes. Your mind retains the image of each picture for about $1/16$ of a second. The image of the bowl is still being retained when the image of the fish is projected to the brain. This causes an overlapping of the pictures in your mind, so the fish appears to be inside the bowl.

Procedure

1. Draw and cut a 4" circle from the poster board.
2. Make 2 holes on each side of the circle with the hole punch. The holes at opposite sides of the poster board should be directly across from each other.
3. Measure and cut two 24" pieces of string.
4. Thread one piece of string through the holes so both ends come out of the same side. Each piece of string should extend out 12". Repeat for the other side.
5. Draw a large empty fishbowl on one side of the circle.
6. Draw a small fish on the center of the other side of the circle.
7. Hold the string and twirl the poster board around in a circle about 15 times in order to twist the string.
8. Pull the string straight out to spin the circle.

20

Anatomy
Lung and Diaphragm

30 minutes

What You Will Do

Model how your lungs and diaphragm work together.

Get it Together

- 16-ounce plastic soda bottle
- 2 9" balloons
- Electrical tape
- Straw
- Canning lid (same diameter as the bottle)
- Modeling clay
- Scissors

Procedure

1. Cut the bottom portion off the bottle.
2. Cut the straw to 5".
3. Tape one balloon to the end of the straw.
4. Suspend the straw through the top bottle opening with clay. Make a tight seal.
5. Cut the narrow end off the second balloon and stretch it over the canning lid.
6. Insert the ring/balloon into the large open end of the soda bottle and seal it with tape.
7. Push and pull on the stretched balloon.

A Closer Look

Your diaphragm is at the bottom of your chest. The stretched balloon represents the diaphragm. The diaphragm contracts and pulls down the bottom of your chest to help you inhale. When you pulled down on the stretched balloon, the inside balloon expanded, or inhaled, air. When you pushed up on the stretched balloon you saw the inside balloon collapse, or exhale.

Attention!
Have an adult cut the bottom off the bottle.

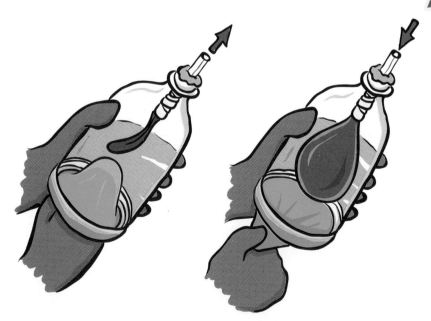

21

Anatomy
Lung Power

15 minutes

What You Will Do

Determine lung capacity.

Get it Together

- Clear glass gallon bottle (cider or vinegar works best)
- Large pan or sink
- 24" plastic or rubber tubing
- Measuring cup
- Masking tape
- Water
- A partner

Procedure

1. Fill the bottle completely with water.
2. Put about 2" of water in the sink.
3. Have your partner place his hand over the mouth of the bottle, covering the top. Then, turn the bottle upside down in the sink, so the mouth of the bottle is underwater.
4. Your partner can remove his hand and no air should enter the bottle. Your partner should continue to hold the inverted bottle over the sink while you start the next step.
5. Insert one end of the tubing into the opening of the bottle.
6. Take a deep breath and blow through the tube as hard as you can. This will empty the air from your lungs into the bottle.
7. Mark the water level on the bottle with a piece of masking tape.
8. Empty the bottle and turn it right-side up.
9. Using a measuring cup, measure the amount of water required to fill the bottle up to your tape mark. This is your lung capacity.

A Closer Look

You used a process called water displacement to determine the amount of air in your lungs. The force of your lungs pushed the water out of the bottle as the air took its place. To get a more accurate reading of your lung capacity, increase your total volume by 20% (multiply your total by 1.2) because you have that much "dead" air still left in your lungs which you cannot expel.

Attention!
The glass bottle full of water is heavy. Do not drop the bottle in the sink; it may break.

22

Reaction Jackson

10 minutes

What You Will Do

Demonstrate human reaction rate.

Get it Together

◆ 12" ruler
◆ A partner

Procedure

1. Have your partner hold the ruler vertically above your open thumb and index finger. The bottom of the ruler should be at the same height as your outstretched fingers.
2. Have your partner drop the ruler without warning.
3. Measure the number at which you catch the ruler.

A Closer Look

The time between when your body senses something and when you actually react is called reaction rate. Different people have different reaction times. Younger people have quicker reaction times than older people.

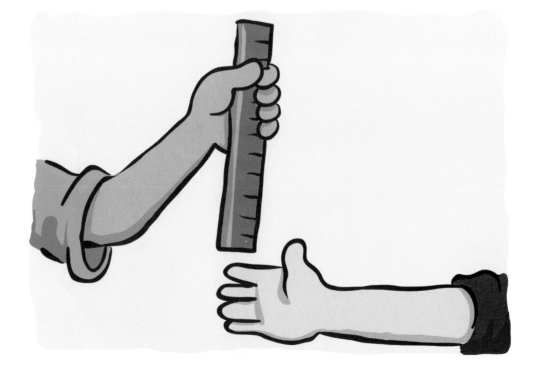

What Now?

Practice this activity to see if you can improve your reaction time.

Anatomy

Seeing Red

2 minutes

What You Will Do

Recognize an afterimage.

Get it Together

◆ Sheet of white paper
◆ Sheet of red paper

Procedure

1. Stare directly at the red paper for about 90 seconds. Do not look at anything else.
2. Now, quickly look at the white paper.

A Closer Look

The white paper should have looked a blue-green color. This is called an afterimage. As you stare at the red color, the cells in your eyes that respond to red get tired. When you switch over to white, your cells subtract the red, leaving the complementary color green behind.

What Now?

Try this with other colors of paper.

24

Skin Sweat

5 minutes

What You Will Do

Determine how sweat cools off the body.

Get it Together

- ◆ Pair of socks
- ◆ Water
- ◆ Warm day

A Closer Look

You sweat when your body gets hot. As sweat evaporates into the air, it cools your body. Likewise, as the water from the sock evaporates into the air, it makes your wet foot feel cooler than your dry foot.

Procedure

1. Dip one sock in water and wring it out so it is only damp.
2. Place the wet sock on one foot and the dry sock on the other.
3. Walk around outside and decide which foot feels cooler.

Anatomy

Snack Time

3 minutes

What You Will Do

Show how saliva begins the digestive process.

Get it Together

- Several unsalted crackers
- Slice of white bread
- Clock
- Water

A Closer Look

The starches found in crackers and bread cannot be immediately used by the body. Enzymes contained in the saliva of your mouth begin the digestion process by breaking down starch into simple sugars. As this breakdown of starch-to-sugar proceeds, the cracker in your mouth starts to taste sweet.

Procedure

1. Take a few bites of the cracker and chew it for one full minute. Notice how the taste changes as it mixes with the saliva in your mouth. Swallow it after one minute of chewing.
2. Take a sip of water to wash out the taste of the cracker.
3. Now repeat Step 1 with the white bread.

What Now?

Try other food products such as meat, fruits, vegetables, etc.

Spinning Like a Top

1 minute

What You Will Do

Illustrate the effects of rapid circular movement.

Get it Together

◆ A partner

Procedure

1. Stand in an open area.
2. Spin quickly for about 20 seconds. Have your partner stay close to you in case to get too dizzy.
3. Sit on the floor.

A Closer Look

The liquid in the semicircular canals of your ears begins to move as your body turns. When your body stops spinning, the liquid continues to move for a few seconds longer. Your brain interpreted this motion as if your body is still spinning. That is why you feel dizzy.

Attention!

Do this activity away from all furniture and sharp objects. Use your partner as a spotter in case you get dizzy.

27

Stereo Vision

5 minutes

What You Will Do

Illustrate how your eyes work together.

Get it Together

◆ Paper

Procedure

Part A: Finger Sausages
1. Put the tips of both index fingers together about 1" from the front of your eyes.
2. Keeping your fingers in this position, close one eye. Do both fingers look the same?
3. Repeat with the other eye closed.

Part B: Hole in the Hand
1. Roll a sheet of paper into a tube about 1" in diameter.
2. Hold the tube over one eye, as if you were looking into a telescope.
3. Hold your free hand in front of the tube, starting about 4" from your eyes.
4. Slowly move your free hand away from, then towards your eyes. Locate the point where you see a hole in your hand.
5. Repeat, switching the tube to your other eye.

A Closer Look

Each eye sends a signal to the brain about what it sees. The brain then takes the messages from both eyes and puts them together into one image. By using one eye, the brain is getting only part of the message. You cannot see an image that lands on your optic nerve. This is called your blind spot. Your brain fills in the blank with information from the other eye. That is why the hole in your hand looks like what you see through the tube.

What Now?

Both you and a partner cover one eye with a patch and play a game of catch with a soft rubber ball. Start at a distance of about 10 feet apart, and slowly increase that distance.

28

Anatomy
The Breath Test

5 minutes+

What You Will Do

Demonstrate the presence of carbon dioxide in exhaled breath.

Get it Together

Part A:
◆ Pickling lime
◆ 2 one-quart clear glass jars with lids
◆ Water
◆ Tablespoon

Part B:
◆ Straw
◆ Clear cup or glass
◆ Water

Procedure

Part A: Making of Limewater
1. Fill one of the jars about ⅔ full of water.
2. Add 1 tablespoon of the pickling lime and stir.
3. Close the jar and allow it to stand, undisturbed, overnight.
4. The next day, pour off the clear liquid into the second jar. Be careful not to pour any of the settled powder into the second jar.
5. The clear liquid in the second jar is an indicator called limewater.

Part B: Testing Your Breath
1. Pour a few ounces of the limewater into the glass.
2. Place the straw at the bottom of the glass and slowly exhale into the limewater. Keep blowing into the straw until the liquid changes colors.

A Closer Look

The liquid turns from clear to a milky white solution. Limewater, a compound that consists of water and calcium atoms, is a chemical indicator that detects the presence of carbon dioxide gas. A chemical reaction occurs when molecules ofcarbon dioxide (which is the gas we exhale after each breath) mix with the limewater.

Attention!
Do not inhale on the straw. Do not taste or drink the limewater.

29

Anatomy
The Eyes, Oh, Those Eyes

3 minutes

What You Will Do

Demonstrate how the human eye works.

Get it Together

- Round glass bowl
- Small lamp without shade
- 12" square black cardboard
- 12" square white cardboard
- Water

- Sharp pencil to make a hole in the cardboard
- Dark room

A Closer Look

The image of the lamp is upside down. This is how the retina in the back of your eye sees an image. Your brain is used to this and can interpret the images so you see them the right way.

Procedure

1. Punch a hole in the center of the black cardboard.
2. Fill the bowl with water.
3. Place the black cardboard on one side of the bowl and the white cardboard on the other side of the bowl. Both cardboard squares should be only a few inches from the bowl.
4. Turn on the lamp and line it up with the two cards.
5. Move the white cardboard back and forth until an image of the lamp appears on it.

Attention!
Use caution to avoid burning yourself on the hot light bulb.

Anatomy
Tongue Twister

10 minutes

What You Will Do

Illustrate how smell affects your sense of taste.

Get it Together

- ◆ Apple
- ◆ Eyedropper
- ◆ Vanilla extract
- ◆ Cotton ball

Procedure

1. Take a bite of the apple, chew it thoroughly, and swallow.
2. Place a few drops of vanilla extract on the cotton ball.
3. Hold the cotton ball near, but not touching, your nose.
4. Take another bite of the apple.

A Closer Look

The apple tastes like vanilla. The taste buds on your tongue allow you to identify only four different basic tastes: Sweet, sour, salty, and bitter. Other taste sensations are partly due to your sense of smell. The vanilla's smell influences how the apple seems to taste.

31

You're a Real Square

5 minutes

What You Will Do

Depict how humans have certain body dimensions that are very similar.

Get it Together

◆ Ball of string
◆ Scissors
◆ A partner

A Closer Look

Your height is the same size as your arm span. This means that your dimensions make a near perfect square. The human body has certain dimensions to ensure proper balance for standing.

Procedure

1. Stand up with your arms stretched out as far as possible.
2. Have your partner cut a piece of string the length of your outstretched arms.
3. Using the same piece of string, measure your height from your head to your toes.

Anatomy
ZZZZZZ's

1 minute

What You Will Do

Demonstrate what makes a person snore.

Get it Together

◆ Wax paper

Procedure

1. Measure and cut an 8" square of wax paper.
2. Hum your favorite song.
3. Place your hands on the sides of the paper and hold it against your lips.
4. Continue to hum the song.

A Closer Look

As you hum into the wax paper, you create vibrations which make sound. Snoring is the sound of the vibration of the soft tissue within the mouth. As you sleep, gravity pulls the tongue and other tissue in the mouth down causing the airway to be partially blocked. As you inhale, air moves through the smaller passage and causes part of the mouth to vibrate. This is snoring.

Birdie, Birdie in the Sky

2 minutes

What You Will Do

Model the physics behind bird flight.

Get it Together

- ◆ 2" x 12" strip of paper
- ◆ Book

Procedure

1. Insert 2" of the paper strip in the center of the book.
2. Hold the book up so the paper is below your mouth.
3. Blow gently across the top of the paper and watch what happens.
4. Now blow harder.

A Closer Look

When air moves over the top of a curved bird, it has farther to go than the air traveling below the bird (where it is flatter). The air above the bird has to move faster to keep up with the air below. This creates a difference in pressure and an upward force known as lift. Airplanes use this same principle to fly.

34

Butterfly Camouflage

10 minutes

What You Will Do

Show how living things adapt to their environment.

Get it Together

◆ Outline of the butterfly (below)
◆ Colored pencils
◆ Paper
◆ Tape
◆ A partner

A Closer Look

Just like your butterfly, living things try to blend in with their environments. This process is called adaptation: the behaviors and appearances of species that help them survive. Every living organism has a variety of adaptations that are suited to its specific surroundings.

Procedure

1. Using the outline at the bottom of this page, trace a butterfly on your paper.
2. Look around the room and pick a spot where you will place your butterfly. The butterfly must be placed completely in the open.
3. Color your butterfly so it will blend in with the spot you choose.
4. Tape your butterfly to its spot.
5. Ask your partner to look for the butterfly. See how long it takes him to find it.

What Now?

Try this experiment with drawings of other living things, such as other insects and small plants.

Earthy Worms

10 minutes

What You Will Do

Determine if earthworms prefer dry or moist conditions.

Get it Together

- 2 earthworms
- Cardboard to cover the top of the container
- Clock or stop watch
- Spray bottle
- Paper towels
- Storage tray container
- Water

Procedure

1. Fold a dry paper towel and place it on the bottom of one side of the tray.
2. Fold a moist paper towel and place it on the other side.
3. Moisten your hands and place the earthworms in the center of the tray making sure that half of each of the worms' bodies rests on the moist paper towel and half rests on the dry towel.
4. Cover the tray with the cardboard. After five minutes, remove the cardboard and observe whether the worms are on the moist or dry surface.

A Closer Look

Earthworms are among the most helpful inhabitants of garden and soil. Earthworms prefer moist surfaces to dry surfaces and tunnel for a living. They eat decayed plant and animal remains in the soil. On damp nights, earthworms come out of their burrows. They crawl on the surface of the ground, seeking leaves and soft fruit to drag underground and eat.

Attention!

Handle the earthworms gently. Keep the worms moist at all times.

What Now?

To determine if earthworms prefer light or dark surfaces, repeat this test using dry towels and cover only half the container with the cardboard. Shine a flashlight over the open half.

36

Goin' Fishing

5 minutes

What You Will Do

Test the effect of temperature on the amount of oxygen.

Get it Together

- ◆ 2 goldfish, same size
- ◆ 2 clear cups or glasses
- ◆ Warm and cold water
- ◆ Clock

Procedure

1. Fill one container with warm water.
2. Place a goldfish in the container.
3. Count the number of times the fish breathes in one minute by counting the number of times the gills move in and out.
4. Return the goldfish to the tank.
5. Fill the second container with cold water.
6. Repeat Steps 2 through 4 with the other goldfish.

A Closer Look

The warm water has less dissolved oxygen in it than the cold water. The goldfish will breathe more often in the warm water in an attempt to take in more oxygen.

Attention!

You will have pet fish after this experiment!

What Now?

Try different species of fish. Try using a larger tank.

37

Going Ape

10 minutes

What You Will Do

Model how primates use a thumb for grasping objects.

Get it Together

- ◆ Tape
- ◆ Several small objects
- ◆ Pencil

Procedure

1. Tape the thumb of your writing hand to your palm so that you cannot move it. The tape should allow your other fingers to move freely.
2. Pick up a pencil with the taped hand and try to write your name.
3. Keep the tape on for 5 minutes and try doing some everyday activities, such as lifting this book, turning the pages, or untying your shoe.
4. Remove the tape and repeat all the activities. Observe the position and action of your thumb and other fingers as you perform each activity.

A Closer Look

You found it difficult to grasp and lift objects when your thumb was taped. The forelimbs of many primates have adaptations for grasping. For example, the human thumb can touch all four fingers. Other mammals like cats, dogs, otters, and seals do not have a thumb for grasping.

Attention!
Do not lift any sharp objects.

Animal Science
Just Ducky

5 minutes

What You Will Do

Demonstrate how ducks stay dry while swimming.

Get it Together

◆ Vegetable shortening
◆ Paper
◆ Scissors
◆ Water
◆ Bowl

Procedure

1. Cut 2 feather shapes from the paper.
2. Coat both sides of one feather with the shortening.
3. Fill the bowl with water.
4. Place both feathers in the water.

A Closer Look

Water soaked into the uncoated feather, but beaded up on the coated feather. The shortening provided a waxy coating that protected the feather. Ducks waterproof their feathers with a waxy type of oil. This oil is produced in a gland at the base of the tail. The duck uses its bill to rub its feathers with oil.

39

Snake in the Grass

1 minute

What You Will Do

Model how snakes feed.

Get it Together

- Grapefruit
- Sock
- Rubber band

Procedure

1. Stretch a sock cuff ("snake") over a grapefruit ("prey") by first pulling on one side and then the other.
2. Work the grapefruit down into the "stomach" of the sock.
3. Remove the grapefruit and put a rubber band around the sock about 3" below the opening.
4. Repeat Steps 1 & 2.

A Closer Look

The rubber band represents the firmly joined jawbones of a snake or lizard. A snake's jawbones can spread apart like the sock cuff. All snakes are meat eaters and some eat large prey. Snakes' jawbones can spread wide apart. In addition, the bones of a snake's skull can move to allow the snake to swallow an animal much larger than itself. Most snakes, however, feed on small rodents, such as mice.

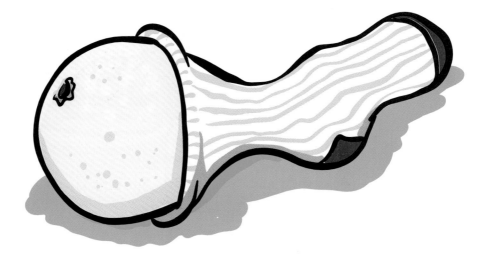

Animal Science
The Bird is the Word

10 minutes

What You Will Do

Make your own birdhouse.

Get it Together

◆ 1$\frac{1}{2}$ ' of rope or thick string
◆ Round one-gallon plastic bottle
◆ Utility knife
◆ Tree

Procedure

1. Rinse the bottle several times. Make sure it is very clean.
2. Have an adult cut out a small circular opening near the bottom of the plastic bottle.
3. Tie one end of the rope around the handle of the bottle and another around the branch of a tree. The tree branch should be thick enough to support the bottle without sagging.
4. Do not disturb your birdhouse.
5. Wait for birds to make a new home.

A Closer Look

Spring time is a good time to provide houses for birds. There is a good chance that a neighborhood bird will find a new home. Do not disturb the home as it will scare away the birds. Watch for babies in the spring.

Attention!
Use caution when working with the knife.

What Now?

Observe the birdhouse and write your observations in journals.

There's Something Fishy

5 minutes

What You Will Do

Observe how fish "breathe."

Get it Together

◆ Several fish in an aquarium

Procedure

1. Closely observe a fish for a few minutes.
2. Watch how frequently the fish opens its mouth.
3. Watch the flaps on each side of the fish's head behind the eyes.
4. Observe the movement of the mouth and flaps at the same time.

A Closer Look

Fish get their oxygen from the water. As a fish swims along, it involuntarily opens its mouth and takes a gulp of water. The water, which contains oxygen, moves through openings in the fish's throat region that leads to the gills. As water flows over the gills, oxygen moves from the water into the fish's blood, while carbon dioxide, a waste product, moves out of the blood and into the water.

What Now?

Help the fish by replenishing their oxygen supply. Scoop a cup of water out of the fish bowl and then pour it back in. Observe the bubbles this creates.

Bacteriology
M is for Mold

2 minutes+

What You Will Do

Observe the growth of mold on bread.

Get it Together

- Resealable sandwich bag
- Slice of white bread
- Spray bottle with water
- Dirty shoe bottom

Procedure

1. Take the slice of bread and brush it against the bottom of your shoe.
2. Spray the bread once with water.
3. Place the bread in the bag and seal it.
4. Place the bread in a warm space and observe it for several days.

A Closer Look

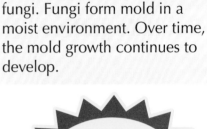

The base of your shoe contains fungi. Fungi form mold in a moist environment. Over time, the mold growth continues to develop.

Attention!
Do not touch the mold.

Clean Up

Throw the bread in the trash.

Nothing to Sneeze At

10 minutes

What You Will Do

Demonstrate how germs spread easily.

Get it Together

- 10 cotton balls
- Round balloon
- Pin
- Windy day outdoors (optional)

Procedure

1. Break each cotton ball into 5 or 6 equal parts.
2. Roll each piece into a puffy little ball.
3. Insert the cotton balls into the balloon through the opening in its neck.
4. Blow up the balloon and tie it at the end.
5. Go outside and hold the balloon in front of you. Pop the balloon with the pin and observe.

A Closer Look

The tiny cotton balls blew away and spread all over, much the same way the germs of a sneeze spread all over a room. This is why it is important to always cover your mouth and use a tissue when you sneeze or cough. It prevents the rapid spread of airborne germs. Also, you should wash your hands to prevent the spread of germs.

Attention!

Use caution when sticking the pin in the balloon.

Clean Up

Gather the cotton balls and balloon pieces and place them in the trash.

44

Chemical Change
How do you Spell Potato?

2 minutes

What You Will Do

Demonstrate that potatoes contain a chemical enzyme.

Get it Together

- 1 cup hydrogen peroxide
- Cut up raw potato
- Clear glass

Procedure

1. Fill the glass about half full of hydrogen peroxide.
2. Add several slices of raw potato. Observe.

A Closer Look

Raw potatoes contain the enzyme catalase. Enzymes promote chemical reactions. Catalase from the potato cells causes the hydrogen peroxide to rapidly break down into water and oxygen gas. This was demonstrated by the bubbling.

Attention!

Use caution when working with hydrogen peroxide. Use only under adult supervision.

45

Chemical Change
Nuclear Energy

2 minutes

What You Will Do

Observe a chain reaction.

Get it Together

◆ 15 dominoes

Procedure

1. Line up 15 dominoes to form a triangle as shown below.
2. Knock over the first domino so that it falls against the second row of dominoes.
3. Set up the dominoes again, but then remove the domino in the third row.
4. Knock over the first domino again.

A Closer Look

In order for a controlled chain reaction to occur, all of the dominoes must be in their proper places. In a nuclear power plant, control rods (dominoes) are also set in a precise order to make sure that the splitting of atoms occurs in a controlled, orderly way. If control rods were not used, the huge amount of energy released during atom splitting could cause an explosion and put people in danger.

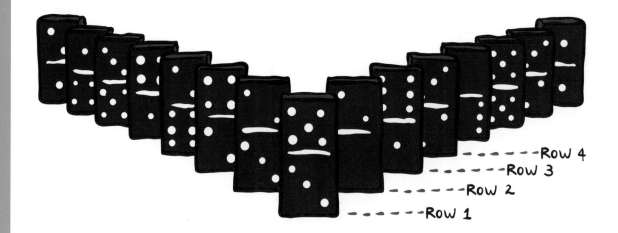

Row 4
Row 3
Row 2
Row 1

46

Chemical Change
Starch Alert

10 minutes

What You Will Do

Demonstrate the presence of starch in foods.

Get it Together

- Dropper bottle of 0.2% solution of iodine
- Sheet of wax paper
- Small sample of each: milk, cracker, cornstarch, sugar, bread, and water
- Toothpicks

Procedure

1. Separate all the food samples on the wax paper.
2. Place 2 drops of iodine solution on each sample.
3. Mix each liquid sample with a clean toothpick.

A Closer Look

When starch is present in a food, the iodine changes color. If a large amount of starch is present, the light brown iodine will turn a deep purple-black color. Lesser amounts of starch will result in a lighter color of purple. This color change results from the chemical bonding between iodine and starch molecules.

Attention!
Iodine stains. Be careful not to get iodine on hands or clothes

Clean Up

Carefully place the wax paper in the trash.

What Now?

Test other foods for starch.

Chemical Change
Yeast Beast

15 minutes

What You Will Do

Display how the presence of sugar affects the activity of yeast.

Get it Together

- ◆ 3 balloons
- ◆ 3 small, narrow-necked bottles
- ◆ Sugar
- ◆ Package of dry yeast
- ◆ Measuring cup
- ◆ Pen
- ◆ Spoon
- ◆ Water

Procedure

1. Gently stretch each balloon so it will inflate easily.
2. Label the bottles A, B, and C.
3. Place a ½ cup of water in each bottle.
4. Put a spoonful of dry yeast in bottle A; a spoonful of sugar in Bottle B; and a spoonful of sugar and yeast in Bottle C.
5. Immediately place a balloon over the openings of the bottles. Make sure the balloons fit tightly around the necks of the bottles.
6. Gently shake the bottles for a few moments.

A Closer Look

The balloon started to inflate in Bottle C because the yeast reacted with the sugar to produce carbon dioxide gas. Nothing happened to the balloons in Bottle A or B because the sugar was separate from the yeast. Yeast cells need the sugar as a food supply. Yeast is used as an important ingredient in the baking of bread, cookies, and cakes because it makes them rise.

Clean Up

Rinse the bottles in running tap water. Catch the yeast particles in the drain trap and dump them in the trash.

Environmental Science
Greenhouse Effect

20 minutes

What You Will Do

Demonstrate the greenhouse effect on our environment.

Get it Together

◆ Thermometer
◆ Automobile
◆ Sunny day

Procedure

1. Take the temperature of the outside air.
2. Have an adult move his car into a sunny location.
3. Close all the windows and place the thermometer on the seat of the car. Allow it to sit in the car for at least 10 minutes.
4. Compare the two temperatures.

A Closer Look

The temperature inside the car was much hotter than the outdoor temperature. The warm air was trapped inside the car without a place to escape. The trapping of heat near the Earth's surface is called the greenhouse effect. Carbon dioxide gas traps much of the heat from the sun. Without this effect, the Earth would be much colder.

Attention!
Do not sit in the car while doing this procedure.

49

Pollution in the Air

3 minutes+

What You Will Do

Show there is pollution in our environment.

Get it Together

- 2 jar lids
- Petroleum jelly
- Paper towels

A Closer Look

Pollution and pollen in the air will settle on the surface of the lid that was on the windowsill. Dirt and dust will stick to the petroleum jelly on contact. The lid in the closed room showed little, if any, pollution.

Procedure

1. Coat the inside of the 2 jar lids with the petroleum jelly.
2. Place one lid on an outside windowsill.
3. Place the other lid somewhere in a closed room.
4. Wait several hours and compare the two lids.

Clean Up

Place the lids in the trash.

What Now?

Keep the lids exposed to the elements for several days and observe the amount of pollution in the air.

Environmental Science
Pollution Solution

3 minutes

What You Will Do

Observe how filtration is used in water purification.

Get it Together

- Liquid, cooled herbal tea in a clear cup
- Coffee filter
- Funnel
- Clear glass
- Crushed charcoal

Procedure

1. Observe the color of the tea.
2. Place the coffee filter into the funnel.
3. Fill it halfway with the crushed charcoal.
4. Place the funnel on top of the glass.
5. Slowly pour the tea through the funnel into the glass.
6. Observe the filtered liquid.

A Closer Look

Your filtered tea was lighter in color than your original tea. The use of charcoal filters is one way to reduce water pollution so it is less harmful to all living things—including humans. In the United States, laws regulate the amount of certain pollutants that can be released into the environment. Federal Laws that control air and water quality are called the Clean Air Act and the Clear Water Act.

Environmental Science
Seeds of Life

60 minutes

What You Will Do

Observe how different seeds are part of your local environment.

Get it Together

- ◆ Several resealable sandwich bags
- ◆ Adult
- ◆ Hand lens

Procedure

1. Ask an adult to accompany you on a seed hunt at a local forest preserve or nature center.
2. When you spot a seed, place a plastic bag over your hand.
3. Turn the bag inside out and gently grab the seed.
4. Return the bag to the original position, and seal it.
5. Gather several different types of seeds.
6. When you get home, use the hand lens to observe the seeds and compare them.
7. Try to determine how each seed is dispersed.

A Closer Look

Seeds are the way plants and trees reproduce. Seeds with fluffy structures are dispersed by the wind. Seeds with sharp burrs are dispersed by attaching themselves to moving creatures and then dropping off at a new location. Dispersals can be caused by wind, water, or living things, including humans.

What Now?

Make a Local Seed Display by mounting your seeds on a large display board.

Environmental Science
Tangled

2 minutes

What You Will Do

Determine the effect of plastic garbage on sea animals.

Get it Together

◆ Rubber band

Procedure

1. Hook one end of the rubber band around your little finger.
2. Stretch the rubber band across the back of your hand and hook the free end to your thumb.
3. Try to remove the rubber band without touching anything.

A Closer Look

You are unable to remove the rubber band. The plastic items in garbage are deadly to sea animals. Seals, fish, and other animals get the plastic rings from 6-pack cans caught around their bodies and cannot remove them. Turtles swallow floating plastic bags because they mistake them for jellyfish. Their digestive tracts become blocked and they die.

What Now?

Cut up plastic can rings and bags and recycle them.

You're All Wet

30 minutes

What You Will Do

Demonstrate how insulation can protect animals from the cold.

Get it Together

- 4 identical glass jars with lids
- 4 thermometers
- Long, narrow strip of dry cloth
- Long, narrow strip of wet cloth
- Pitcher of hot tap water
- Leaves

- Refrigerator
- Watch
- Marker
- Paper
- Pencil
- A partner

Procedure

1. Label Jar 1 *Leaves*, Jar 2 *Dry Cloth*, Jar 3 *Wet Cloth*, and Jar 4 *Control*.
2. On a sheet of paper, write: Temperature 0 minutes, Temperature 10 minutes, Temperature 20 minutes, Temperature 30 minutes. Do this for each jar.
3. Have your partner take the temperature of the hot water in the pitcher. Write that temperature under *Temperature 0 minutes* for all four jars.
4. Pour equal amounts of water in each of the jars. Place the lids on the jars.
5. Wrap the jar labeled *Wet Cloth* with the wet cloth and the jar labeled *Dry Cloth* with the dry cloth.
6. Place all four jars in the refrigerator, leaving space around each one.
7. Stack leaves around the jar labeled *Leaves*.
8. Every 10 minutes, have your partner take the temperature of the water in each jar. As your partner calls out the temperatures, record them on your sheet.
9. After 30 minutes, record the final temperatures, then list the jars in order from warmest to coldest.

A Closer Look

Since you did nothing to the control jar, you can use it to compare the temperatures in the other jars. The dry cloth provides good insulation, much like an animal's coat. The water in this jar stayed the warmest compared to your control jar. The wet cloth actually stole heat from the water inside its jar, as the water from the cloth evaporated into the air. This jar was the coldest compared to your control jar. The leaves may have offered a little insulation, so the water in this jar may be slightly warmer than your control jar. Conclusion? Stay covered in dry clothes to protect yourself from the cold.

54

Heat Energy
Keeping Warm

15 minutes

What You Will Do

Analyze how heavy fabrics keep people warm.

Get it Together

- Small bowl
- 6" x 6" thin piece of cotton
- 6" x 6" thick piece of heavy wool
- 3 ice cubes

Procedure

1. Place an ice cube in a bowl.
2. Wrap one ice cube in cotton.
3. Wrap one ice cube in wool.
4. Allow them to sit for 10 minutes.
5. Unwrap the ice cubes in the cotton and wool.
6. Compare the size of the ice cubes.

A Closer Look

The ice cube in the wool fabric did not melt as fast as the ice cube covered in cotton because wool is a better insulator than cotton. The ice cube in the bowl melted the fastest because it had no protection. The wool fabric is more effective at keeping the warm air away from the ice. This is why material like wool is needed to keep body heat in and the cold air out.

Cotton

Wool

Pick a Penny

2 minutes

What You Will Do

Demonstrate how the human body conducts heat.

Get it Together

- 5 copper coins, each with a different date
- Plate
- Hat
- Several partners

A Closer Look

This little "magic trick" is not really magic. Metal conducts heat very easily. When the hands held the copper penny, the metal absorbed the body heat. As this penny is warmer, it is easy to pick it out from the remaining coins that are at room temperature.

Procedure

1. Place the pennies on the plate and have a partner read the dates.
2. Ask your partner to pick out one penny and look at the date.
3. Have the group pass it around until each person has checked the date.
4. Promptly put all the pennies in a hat and shake them.
5. Reach in the hat and feel around for the penny that is the warmest. Surprise your partners by pulling out the penny they picked!

Heat Energy
Sun Power

1 minute

What You Will Do

Show that energy is derived from the sun.

Get it Together

◆ Solar-powered calculator (non-battery type)

Procedure

1. Place the calculator in direct sunlight beside a window or outdoors.
2. Turn on the calculator and cover the solar cells with your finger. Observe the display.
3. Uncover the solar cells and observe the display.
4. Now cover all but one of the solar cells. What happens?

A Closer Look

Your calculator uses light from the sun as its source of energy. Block the light source and there is no display of numbers. Nearly all living things obtain energy either directly or indirectly from the energy of sunlight captured during a process called photosynthesis. During photosynthesis, light energy is changed into food energy.

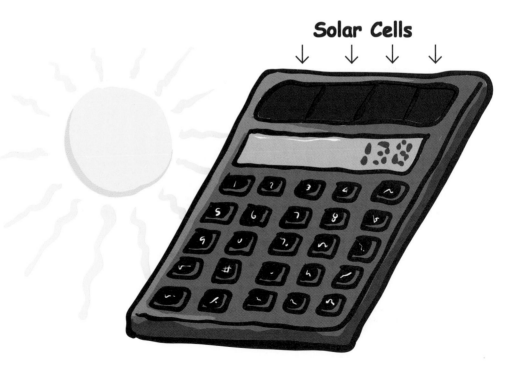

Solar Cells

Plant Science

Don't Sponge off Me

1 minute

What You Will Do

Compare a natural and a synthetic sponge.

Get it Together

◆ Natural sponge
◆ Synthetic sponge
◆ Magnifying glass

Procedure

1. Examine a natural sponge, and then look at it through the magnifying glass. Look carefully at the holes.
2. Repeat Step 1 with the synthetic sponge.

Plant Science

Fruit or Vegetable?

10 minutes

What You Will Do

Observe specific characteristics of angiosperms.

Get it Together

- ◆ Hand lens or magnifying glass
- ◆ Knife
- ◆ Several different types of fruit such as apples, cherries, peaches, plums, tomatoes, or peppers

Procedure

1. Use the lens to carefully observe the outside of each fruit for color, odor, size, and shape.
2. Carefully cut each fruit in half.
3. Observe each fruit's color, odor, shape, size again.
4. Count the number of seeds in each.
5. Eat each fruit and notice the taste difference.

A Closer Look

You may not think that vegetables such as tomatoes and peppers are actually classified as fruits. Fruits contain seeds and have a fleshy, edible part. They vary in color, shape, and the number of seeds they contain. An angiosperm is a plant that produces seeds that are enclosed in a fruit. Angiosperms produce both flowers and fruits.

Attention!
Use caution when cutting fruits with the knife.

Plant Science
It's in the Bag

1 minute+

What You Will Do

Display the process of transpiration.

Get it Together

◆ Sandwich bag
◆ Plant with leaves
◆ String

Procedure

1. Without removing leaves from the plant, place the bag over several leaves.
2. Seal the bottom of the bag carefully with the string. Do not harm the stem of the plant.
3. Remove the bag in 24 hours and observe the inside.

A Closer Look

Water enters a plant through its roots. It travels up the stem and into the leaves. Water exits a plant through the leaves in a process called "transpiration." Heat energy is taken from the air to help evaporate the water from the leaves. In this case, the water could not evaporate since it got trapped in the bag.

What Now?

Try different types of trees or different sized leaves.

Multicolored Flowers

5 minutes+

What You Will Do

Observe the process of plant nourishment.

Get it Together

- 4 clear glasses
- Scissors
- 4 colors of food coloring
- 4 fresh white carnations
- Water
- Warm room

Procedure

1. Pour about 2" of water into each glass.
2. Add 2-3 drops of a different food coloring to each of the glasses.
3. With your scissors, trim the flowers to 2" taller than the glasses.
4. Cut along the stem of the flowers to split them in half lengthwise. Make about a 2" cut.
5. Place one flower in each glass.
6. Leave the flowers in a warm room for a few hours.

A Closer Look

The white flowers turn the same color as the food coloring. The top of the plant actually pulls water up the stem from the bottom part of the plant. From here, the water spreads across the whole flower.

Attention!

Food coloring stains clothing. Use caution with the scissors.

Plant Science
Nature's Eggs

50 minutes

What You Will Do

Demonstrate how plant material can be used for dye.

Get it Together

- One cup of colorful plants (blackberries, red cabbage, cranberries, beets, spinach, etc.)
- 1 Tbsp. vinegar
- Water
- Pan
- Stove
- 2-3 hardboiled eggs

A Closer Look

The boiling water helps extract, or draw out, the color from the plants. The vinegar, which is a weak acid, helps the food-coloring bind to the eggs.

Procedure

1. Place the plants and eggs in the pan.
2. Add enough water to cover the plants and eggs.
3. Add the vinegar.
4. Bring the water to a boil and let simmer for 20 minutes.
5. Remove from heat and let stand for 20 minutes.

Attention!
Use caution when heating the water and eggs.

Plant Science
Super Beans

1 minute+

What You Will Do

Display the water absorbency of dried beans.

Get it Together

- ◆ Bag of dried beans (pinto, lima, kidney, etc.)
- ◆ Glass
- ◆ Water

A Closer Look

Like most dried seeds, beans get bigger when placed in water because the water molecules seep through the walls of the seeds. As they swell, seeds push out of the glass with great force.

Procedure

1. Fill the glass to the top with the beans.
2. Add water to the brim of the glass.
3. Allow the glass to sit for several hours.

Clean Up

Cook the beans and eat them if desired.

Plant Science
The Good Seeds

3 minutes+

What You Will Do

Demonstrate that seeds will sprout without soil.

Get it Together

- ◆ Any type of seed
- ◆ Wet paper towel
- ◆ Dry paper towel
- ◆ 2 plastic, resealable bags

Procedure

1. Wrap several seeds in the wet paper towel.
2. Place them in the bag and seal the bag.
3. Wrap several seeds in the dry paper towel.
4. Place them in the second bag and seal the bag.
5. Observe both bags in several days.

A Closer Look

The seeds in the wet bag will begin to sprout while the seeds in the dry bag do not sprout. This is because water is the key ingredient needed for growth of all living things. Soil is not needed for the seeds to start the growth process.

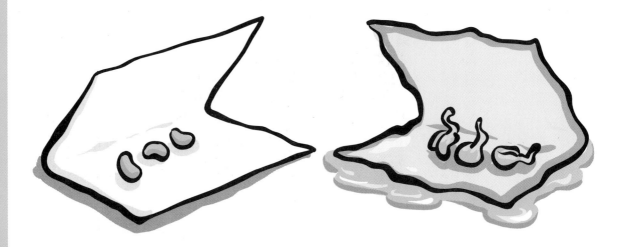

What Now?

Continue to allow the seeds to grow, then slice open and examine the seeds.